KETANJI BROWN JACKSON
A JUSTICE FOR ALL

TO ALL THE BOLD MOTHERS (AND MOTHER FIGURES)
WHO PAVE PATHS AND BREAK MOLDS FOR GENERATIONS TO FOLLOW.
I SEE YOU. ALSO TO MY OWN MAMA—JENNIFER CARLISLE-PETERS. I RISE BECAUSE OF YOU.
—T. C.

FOR MY MUM, PAUL, WOLFGANG, AND ALL THOSE WHO PERSEVERE.
—J. S.

SIMON & SCHUSTER BOOKS FOR YOUNG READERS
An imprint of Simon & Schuster Children's Publishing Division
1230 Avenue of the Americas, New York, New York 10020
Text © 2023 by Tami Charles
Illustration © 2023 by Jemma Skidmore
Book design by Lucy Ruth Cummins © 2023 by Simon & Schuster, Inc.
For information about special discounts for bulk purchases, please contact Simon & Schuster Special Sales at
1-866-506-1949 or business@simonandschuster.com.
The Simon & Schuster Speakers Bureau can bring authors to your live event. For more information or to book an event,
contact the Simon & Schuster Speakers Bureau at 1-866-248-3049 or visit our website at www.simonspeakers.com.
The text for this book was set in Lust Text.
The illustrations for this book were rendered in gouache and wax pencil.
Manufactured in the United States of America
0223 LAK
First Edition
2 4 6 8 10 9 7 5 3 1
Library of Congress Cataloging-in-Publication Data
Names: Charles, Tami, author. | Skidmore, Jemma, illustrator.
Title: Ketanji Brown Jackson : a justice for all / Tami Charles ; illustrated by Jemma Skidmore.
Description: First edition. | New York : Simon & Schuster Books for Young Readers, 2023. | Includes bibliographical
references. | Audience: Ages 4-8. | Audience: Grades K-1. | Summary: "Discover the incredible story of Justice Ketanji
Brown Jackson, who followed her childhood dream of becoming a lawyer and eventually became the first Black
woman to sit on the US Supreme Court in this picture book biography."— Provided by publisher.
Identifiers: LCCN 2022041862 (print) | LCCN 2022041863 (ebook) |
ISBN 9781665935265 (hardcover) | ISBN 9781665935272 (ebook)
Subjects: LCSH: Jackson, Ketanji Brown, 1970- —Juvenile literature. | Judges—United States.—Juvenile literature. |
United States. Supreme Court—Juvenile literature. | LCGFT: Picture books.
Classification: LCC KF8745.J25 C48 2023 (print) | LCC KF8745.J25 (ebook) | DDC 347.73/2634 [B]—dc23/eng/20220921
LC record available at https://lccn.loc.gov/2022041862
LC ebook record available at https://lccn.loc.gov/2022041863

KETANJI BROWN JACKSON
A JUSTICE FOR ALL

WRITTEN BY TAMI CHARLES · ILLUSTRATED BY JEMMA SKIDMORE

SIMON & SCHUSTER BOOKS FOR YOUNG READERS

NEW YORK   LONDON   TORONTO   SYDNEY   NEW DELHI

EVERY DREAM BEGINS
WITH THE SMALLEST STEP.

And I'm feeling bold today!

Up up up

I CLIMB . . .

past columns so tall,
they could almost
touch the sky.

232 years of history
held within these walls,
and here I stand,
wondering if one day
I could sit
on the highest court in the land.

Mama whispers:
"You absolutely can . . .

protect the people
and the Constitution."

SINCE 1790,
115 justices have done just that.
Mostly men
mostly white
only six women,
though none have been Black . . .
until now.

Cameras flash
	as the whole world watches,
		curious about the woman in blue
			who rocks sisterlocks.
			She's earned this spot,
				the first Black female Supreme Court justice . . .
		2022.

			With her right hand
				held high,

					she takes an oath,
						ready.

					And so begins the day
						when the world meets
							the woman who's studied,
								pushed,
									and prepared for this moment
										her whole life:

KETANJI
ONYIKA

"Meaning 'lovely one,'"
	Mama says. . . .

"But today we'll know her as
historymaker,
barrier breaker,
her journey's long begun. . . ."

The story of how she arrived
at this seat,
at this table,
on this special day

was built upon ancestors' dreams,
intentional
and courageous in every way. . . .

400 YEARS AGO,
before we knew
that a girl with an African name
would change the face
of the Supreme Court,

her ancestors worked
and dreamed and

d
a
n
c
e
d

beneath wide-open skies.

UNTIL ONE DAY . . .
their freedom was
stolen,
gone,
taken away.

From the moment
they arrived on American soil,
they fought to change
the fabric of this country . . .

with their hearts
and their words,
with their silence
and their songs,

because denying freedom
to anyone,
no matter their color,
is wrong.

These are the hopes
and the dreams from which
Ketanji Onyika Brown
was born.

1970S MIAMI.

Palm trees
sway in the breeze

as the little girl
with a crown of curls
colors next to her father,

who is studying the laws of this land,
and her mother,
who is grading papers by hand.

Proud daughter of
a lawyer and a principal,
who both attended
segregated schools.

Descendant of
ancestors once forbidden
to read,
to learn,
to vote.

Together, they sowed seeds
of a future without limits . . .

one where barriers
were knocked down,
paths were made clear,
because *here*
in America,
Ketanji's parents
and ancestors demanded
opportunities and equality for all.

1980S.

A teenager now.
Honor student.
Star of the debate team.

Ketanji works hard
and travels the country,
sweeping competitions;
her speeches on
justice and fairness
are hard to beat.

Visions of Harvard
bloom at Ketanji's feet.
At school, a guidance counselor suggests
she set her sights low.

But what happens
when you tell a girl with dreams *NO*?

WE
BELONG
HERE

NO ROOM
FOR
RACISM

NO
MORE

NO ☒
MORE

SHE
RISES
ANYWAY!

Past classroom walls
and library halls,
growing,
learning,
protesting.
Liberty is for ALL!

HAR

H

HARVARD

Ketanji doesn't limit herself.
She tries her hand at new things:
acting, knitting, singing,

making room in
her heart
for new friends
and even . . .

LOVE.

1990S BOSTON.

Ketanji's journey is far from done.
From classrooms to courtrooms,
there are more steps to take,
bigger moves to make.

              up
        up
Up

she continues to rise!

By the early 2000s,
Ketanji knows the kind of lawyer
she wants to be . . .

one who uses facts—
not arguments—
to persuade,
to find solutions
that are reasonable and just.

LOVING V. VIRGINIA

BROWN V. BOARD OF EDUCATION

CIVIL RIGHTS ACT OF 1964

As a law clerk,
there are long days
and even longer nights
researching,
writing,
preparing cases at twilight.

As a public defender,
she works to show
how cruel it is
to push people
to plead guilty
to crimes they
are innocent of.

Optimistic,
realistic,
Ketanji is known for being fair
and dedicated to the people
and the Constitution.

She rises even higher,
becoming a judge of the circuit court,
where she rules
to protect immigrants
and workers' rights.

Ketanji is on a mission!

She follows in the footsteps of the heroes who came before her:

Charlotte E. Ray

Jane Bolin

Constance Baker Motley

All supremely qualified,
yet because of prejudice
denied
a chance
to sit on the
highest court in the land.

Still Ketanji set her sights higher,
knowing the steps they took
gave her wings to soar
and want more
for herself,
the people,
this land.

Because of their sacrifice,
she absolutely can
become the FIRST.

Ketanji isn't the only one who believed—her daughters did too.

And so did the president. . . .

"For too long, our government,
our courts haven't looked like America. . . .
It's time that we have a Court
that reflects the full talents and
greatness of our nation. . . ."

All Ketanji needed was
enough Senate votes
to make her dream come true.

2022 WASHINGTON, DC.

History is finally made
as Ketanji sits before the Senate.

Cameras flash
through questions asked,

each one designed
to shake her,
break her,
but Judge Jackson
knows her worth
and her work.

Hard questions don't scare her one bit!

"I was born in this great nation . . . ,"
she declares.
"I love our country
and the Constitution
and the rights that make us free."

With her head held high,
Ketanji dreams out loud
for all to see.

And the senators agree!

232 YEARS.

Never before have we seen
a Supreme Court judge
quite like her.

This opportunity is for the taking,
centuries in the making!

"I am also ever buoyed by the
leadership of generations past
who helped to light the way.
They . . . did the heavy lifting
that made this day possible."

The voice of a nation,
she is you,
she is me,

blazing a trail
for the future:

the justices,
the changemakers,
the pioneers

who'll remember this year
with great pride!

So as cameras flash,
of course
I rise,
I rejoice,
I smile!

(Wouldn't you?)

If you witnessed history
and
saw the American
dream come true?

KETANJI ONYIKA BROWN JACKSON,

justice for the
highest court in the land. . . .

And now,
because of *them*,
because of *her*,
I know one day
I will
and
certainly can!

AUTHOR'S NOTE

IN 232 YEARS AND 115 APPOINTMENTS, our nation never had a Black woman selected to serve on the Supreme Court of the United States. That changed on February 25, 2022, when President Joseph R. Biden announced his nominee for the 116th Associate Justice. He wanted a candidate who was dedicated to upholding the law, a person of good character who understood how Supreme Court decisions affect American lives. Most important, he wanted to break the unwritten rules and traditions that prevented African American women from sitting on the highest court in the land.

In a press conference to announce the retirement of Justice Stephen Breyer and the nominee to be his replacement, President Biden declared, "The person I will nominate will be someone with extraordinary qualifications, character, experience, and integrity. And that person will be the first Black woman ever nominated to the United States Supreme Court. It's long overdue, in my view."

Ketanji Brown Jackson met and surpassed the president's criteria. Many people believed in her, especially her daughter Leila. In 2016, at the age of eleven, Leila wrote to then-president Barack Obama to ask that he consider her mom for the Supreme Court. While Ketanji wasn't selected at the time, she was eventually nominated by President Biden.

Born in 1970 in Washington, DC, Ketanji moved to Miami, Florida, as a girl. There, her father studied to become a lawyer, and her mother, a teacher, eventually became a magnet school principal. Both of her parents attended segregated schools and were the first in their families to graduate from college. Ketanji has spoken of the intriguing history of her family: her ancestors on both sides were enslaved; her grandparents were raised in Georgia, where discrimination and prejudice were widespread; and her mother is a master fiber artist in crocheting and knitting, skills that Ketanji became quite good at in her adult years.

Growing up, Ketanji excelled in school, both academically and in extracurricular activities. She served as class president of Miami Palmetto Senior High School and was a star of the speech and debate team. While most team events took place in Florida, students sometimes flew to Ivy League campuses for national competitions. This is how Ketanji fell in love with Harvard University.

When it was time to apply to college, a school counselor cautioned her to set her sights low. But that didn't stop Ketanji. She was so certain of her goals that she wrote them in her senior yearbook: "I want to go into law and eventually have a judicial appointment."

And that she did!

Ketanji would go on to graduate from both Harvard University and Harvard Law School, though she often had to fight injustice along the way. During one incident on campus, a fellow student displayed a Confederate flag, which African American students interpreted as a message that they didn't belong at Harvard. Ketanji sprang into action with her classmates, organizing rallies and silent protests while refusing to be distracted from her studies.

Over the course of her career, she served many roles, including clerk, federal public defender, private lawyer, district court judge, vice chair and commissioner of the U.S. Sentencing Commission, and, most recently, U.S. court of appeals judge, before securing the Supreme Court nomination.

Being nominated didn't mean that Ketanji would automatically be offered the job. There were four days of confirmation hearings, during which people would testify on Ketanji's behalf and senators would question her about her work, her beliefs, and her goals to uphold the law. Then the Senate would vote.

March 21, 2022, marked the first day of the confirmation hearings. As Ketanji spoke about her career and motherhood, *New York Times* photographer Sarahbeth Maney captured an image that quickly went viral. In it, seventeen-year-old Leila Jackson looks at her mother with loving pride.

As a picture book author and reader, I've often seen books in which a parent lovingly admires their child, but rarely do I get a perspective from the other way around. I wrote this book to shine a light on the pride children feel when they witness loved ones following their own dreams. In this case, I chose to spotlight a girl who represents the Leila Jackson within us all. May this book remind us to honor the greatness of those who've come before us and to see our potential to soar to new heights because of them.

IMPORTANT DATES

September 14, 1970: Born in Washington, DC, to parents who attended segregated schools and went on to attend historically Black colleges, becoming a lawyer (her father) and an elementary school principal (her mother).

1988: Graduates from Miami Palmetto Senior High School.

1992: Graduates with honors from Harvard University.

1996: Graduates from Harvard Law School. Marries fellow Harvard graduate Dr. Patrick Graves Jackson.

1999: Serves as clerk for Supreme Court Justice Stephen Breyer, whom she later replaces upon his retirement.

2000: Begins working for a private law firm in Boston. Daughter Talia born.

2004: Daughter Leila born.

2005: Becomes a federal public defender in Washington, DC.

2009: Appointed by President Barack Obama to serve as vice chair of the U.S. Sentencing Commission.

2012: Nominated by President Obama to the U.S. District Court for the District of Columbia.

February 25, 2022: Nominated by President Biden to serve as the 116th Associate Justice of the U.S. Supreme Court, making history as the first Black woman to fill this role.

April 7, 2022: With a Senate vote of 53 yeses and 47 noes, Ketanji Brown Jackson is officially confirmed as Associate Justice to the Supreme Court.

IMPORTANT PEOPLE AND HISTORY SHOWN IN THE ART

CHARLOTTE E. RAY (1850–1911)

Charlotte E. Ray was the first Black female lawyer in the United States. A graduate of Howard University, she received her law degree in 1872 and was admitted to the District of Columbia bar, making her the first woman member, as well as the first Black woman certified as a lawyer in the United States. Though she attempted to maintain a law office in Washington, DC, she experienced much prejudice and became a teacher.

JANE BOLIN (1908–2007)

Jane Bolin was the first Black woman to graduate from Yale Law School, in 1931. In 1939, she became the first Black female judge in the United States.

CONSTANCE BAKER MOTLEY (1921–2005)

Constance Motley was a civil rights lawyer who graduated from Columbia University. She made history when she became the first Black woman to argue a case before the Supreme Court. In total, she argued ten Supreme Court cases, winning nine of them. She is also known for her work on *Brown v. Board of Education*, which was a landmark case that led to the end of school segregation. In the 1960s, Justice Motley was in the running for Supreme Court justice, but ultimately she was not selected—some suspected due to her race and gender. In 1966, President Lyndon B. Johnson selected her as a federal court judge—the first Black woman to earn this position.

CIVIL RIGHTS ACT OF 1964

A landmark law that protected the right to vote and outlawed segregation in all public spaces, such as theaters, restaurants, and parks.

LOVING V. VIRGINIA

An important civil rights case decided on June 12, 1967, in which the Supreme Court ruled that banning interracial marriage is unconstitutional. Every year on June 12, Loving Day is celebrated to honor Mildred and Richard Loving, who filed the original suit, as well as interracial families in America.

BIBLIOGRAPHY

Britannica Kids. "Brown v. Board of Education of Topeka." Accessed May 28, 2022. kids.britannica.com/kids/article/Brown-v-Board-of -Education-of-Topeka/627788.

Britannica Kids. "Civil Rights Act." Accessed May 28, 2022. kids.britannica.com/kids/article/Civil-Rights-Act/632760#:~:text=The%20 Civil%20Rights%20Act%20was,U.S.%20laws%20on%20civil%20rights.

CBS. "Getting to Know SCOTUS Nominee Ketanji Brown Jackson." *CBS Sunday Morning*, March 20, 2022. youtube.com/watch?v=bYhH5J _LYzg&t=58s.

The Editors of Encyclopaedia Britannica. "Charlotte E. Ray." *Encyclopaedia Britannica*. Accessed May 28, 2022. britannica.com/biography /Charlotte-E-Ray.

Fisher, Mark, Ann E. Marimow, and Lori Rozsa. "How Ketanji Brown Jackson Found a Path between Confrontation and Compromise." *Washington Post*, February 25, 2022. washingtonpost.com/politics/2022/02/25/ketanji-brown-jackson-miami-family-parents.

Laws.com. "Loving v. Virginia." Last modified October 9, 2020. kids.laws.com/loving-v-virginia.

Martin, Douglas. "Jane Bolin, the Country's First Black Woman to Become a Judge, Is Dead at 98." *New York Times*, January 10, 2007. nytimes.com/2007/01/10/obituaries/10bolin.html.

Mazzei, Patricia. "How a High School Debate Team Shaped Ketanji Brown Jackson." *New York Times*, February 26, 2022. nytimes .com/2022/02/26/us/ketanji-brown-jackson-high-school-debate.html.

NPR. "After 232 Years, Ketanji Brown Jackson Is the First Black Woman on the Supreme Court." *Weekend Edition Sunday*, April 10, 2022. npr .org/2022/04/10/1091927625/after-232-years-ketanji-brown-jackson-is-the-first-black-woman-on-the-supreme-co#:~:text= Ketanji%20Brown%20Jackson%2C%20speaking%20at,Court%20of%20the%20United%20States.&text=KETANJI%20BROWN%20 JACKSON%3A%20But%20we've%20made%20it.

PBS. "Judge Ketanji Brown Jackson Supreme Court confirmation hearings—Day 1." *PBS News Hour*, March 21, 2022. pbs.org/newshour /politics/watch-live-judge-ketanji-brown-jackson-supreme-court-confirmation-hearings-day-1.

Southern Poverty Law Center. "Ketanji Brown Jackson: Legal career timeline." April 7, 2022. splcenter.org/news/2022/04/07 /ketanji-brown-jackson-legal-career-timeline.

United States Courts. "Constance Baker Motley: Judiciary's Unsung Rights Hero." February 20, 2020. uscourts.gov/news/2020/02/20 /constance-baker-motley-judiciarys-unsung-rights-hero.

The White House. "The Senate Confirms Ketanji Brown Jackson to Serve on the U.S. Supreme Court." whitehouse.gov/kbj.